WHEN LONELINESS VISITS

BY KEAH L. MASON

PURPOSED PUBLISHING COMPANY, LLC

When Loneliness Visits

ISBN: 978-0-578-84852-5

Library of Congress Control Number: 2021901623

Published by Purposed Publishing Company, LLC

www.purposedpublishingcompany.com

Email inquiries to: info@purposedpublishingcompany.com

Printed in the United States of America

Cover designed by Stephen Fortune at Skycon Media, LLC

Editing by Monica Settles

Proofreading by Jessica P. Hill at Hilltop Management and Consulting

TABLE OF CONTENTS

In Celebration....4

Dear Reader: Walk with Me....5

Part I - Company's Coming....7

- Chapter 1 - Meet the Girls....8
- Chapter 2 - What is Loneliness?....15
- Chapter 3 - Pieces of Me....19

Part II - Company's Here: Understanding Our Behaviors and Actions....24

- Chapter 4 - Lies and Negative Self-Talk....25
- Chapter 5 - Isolation....33
- Chapter 6 - Toxic Behavior....37

Part III - Be My Guest: A New Perspective....52

- Chapter 7 - Revelation....57
- Chapter 8 - Intentionality....69
- Chapter 9 - Self-Discovery....79

Meet the Author....86

In Celebration

I wear your clothes because I wanna be as fly as you.
I wear your shoes because I wanna walk like you.
I wear your jewelry because you're the queen of my heart.
Your furniture makes my house feel like a home, where you'll always be with me.
When I open my mouth to speak, I hear you.
When I look in the mirror, I see your reflection.
The tattoo on my arm displays our two hearts with a line that signals always.
I am always your daughter. You are always my mother.
I love you, Mommy.
And your forever response will be heard in my heart, "I love you, more."
Rest well, my sweet girl.
Kathryn Anita Mason
July 13, 1958 – May 29, 2020

Dear Reader: Walk with Me

I am getting ready to take a journey, and I would like for you to join me. Going back down memory lane can sometimes be dark and uncomfortable, and I don't want to do it alone. I'm about to revisit some choices I've made and experiences that didn't feel so good, and I would appreciate your presence with me.

My journey may look a lot like yours, or perhaps it is a bit different than yours, but you'll see that we have a common outcome. At some point in our lives, we have a common visitor: loneliness. Loneliness can be a frequent or infrequent visitor in our lives, and we all deal with it in many ways when it arrives. That's why I'd love for us to walk together. I want you to reflect with me about our loneliness and look at how it has affected our actions and behaviors. Let us see how we sometimes dressed ourselves in the negative thoughts associated with feeling lonely. We are going to uncover some truths about how loneliness has impacted us in seasons when its company wasn't welcomed in our lives. We will uproot these things together because none of us must face it alone.

Once we get past the weeds, let us discover a different path we can take. A new perspective on loneliness will be our tour guide. As we strive to take another path to view loneliness through a new lens, let us embrace our experiences with it along the way and allow them to be our greatest lessons. We will find that we can, in fact change our perspective and response to loneliness as we dress ourselves in its truth of how it should be seen. Our greatest pains in dealing with loneliness may ultimately lead us to new discoveries in how we respond to it, changing our view of loneliness from unwelcomed to at times, necessary.

In this book, I would like to share with you how I have dealt with loneliness, and allow you to share your experiences, too. By now, I feel like loneliness is either written on my forehead or tattooed across my chest. I may even speak the language fluently. Although it's a heavy burden at times, I will share my struggles as I transparently discuss the negative things that loneliness has led me to and how I have learned to deal with it in a positive and healthy way.

Loneliness can lead to negative thinking and behaviors in our lives, but only if that is what we allow. It does not have to be all darkness and oppression. It's not just Maxwell's "Lonely's The Only Company" playing on repeat. I'll share how loneliness led me to lies, negative self-talk, isolation, and toxic behavior. I'll show you my struggles, my falls, and my failures, but I'll also share the other side - the good side. I will show you how it eventually led me to healing, intentionality, and self-discovery. As I share my story, and as you and I talk and reflect along the way, I hope that you, too, will confront and overcome your struggles with loneliness.

I am so happy you are here with me. Let's get started on this journey.

With Love and Courage,

Keah

PART I

COMPANY'S COMING

Chapter 1
Meet the Girls

One of the most important things we can do to start is to first uncover who we are and connect our truths. So, come along as we take an intense look at ourselves. Let's unpack some of our stories as we meet the ladies below. You may see yourself in one or more of these women. I, too, am one of these women.

The Ladies	
Samantha: The Social Butterfly	Meet Samantha. She has good girlfriends who all love to spend time together. From lunch dates, Zumba classes, movie nights, and weekend getaways, Samantha has always kicked it with her girls. Daily phone conversations with them were the norm for her. Birthday celebrations, comedy shows, and Jazz festivals were always part of their plans; but, as life would have it, seasons changed. Samantha's social calendar isn't filled anymore. Her social life with her friends is now limited to likes and maybe a few comments on Facebook and Instagram. Her friends just simply got busy, so now, lonely is her only company.

Victoria: The Empty Nester	Victoria is the super mom. She traded in her two-seater convertible over two decades ago for a minivan. She got used to being a soccer mom, and she fully embraced that role. Uber drivers can't hold a candle to her. Always on the road, she takes her kids to various sporting events, movie dates, game nights, choir practice, and competitions. Her house was the spot for her kids' friends, and she busied herself washing loads of laundry and serving snacks to the hungry household. She loved that life. However, life moved on and now her babies aren't babies anymore. They are grown and busy, leaving her as an empty nester, and now she's alone. What is she supposed to do now that she's not taking care of her family?
Natasha: Married but Single?	Natasha has been married for ten years. It wasn't long into her marriage when the date nights faded, and family time became limited to holidays and special occasions. Breakfast is a rushed cup of coffee in silence while scrolling through e-mail messages. Dinner is a party of one because her husband spends late nights at the office putting in overtime. Natasha is so over it. Lying beside the man of her dreams each night doesn't satisfy her need for connection and companionship. He is such a great provider, but he doesn't have any quality time for her.

Belinda: The Retiree	Belinda had a fulfilling career and has accomplished all her dreams. From climbing the corporate ladder, to mentoring others, she experienced a great deal of success. Now that she is retired, life has slowed down for her. What else is there for her to do? Her life was always so focused on her career. So, now what? She has hobbies, but life is awfully quiet now. She often feels lonely and finds herself wishing she had something to do.
LaShay: The Boss Chic	LaShay, an educated and very successful high achiever is completely confident in her job. Her work ethic is off the chain. She is highly valued and respected and is the go-to person for various tasks. But when was the last time she was invited out to lunch with her coworkers? No invites to happy hours, holiday parties, or anything. How is the most successful woman in the office also the loneliest?
Mariana: Uninvited Moms Club	Mariana exchanged her career driven life for the role of wife and mommy. She's busy taking care of her little ones, or so everyone assumes. Because she has this great deal of responsibility at home, her friends and family assume she's too busy to hang out. She doesn't have time to kick it with the girls anymore, right? Yep, that's what everyone thinks, and no one bothers to call just to talk or to ask if she'd like to hang out. Although

	she is extremely busy and doesn't have much time for the social life that she misses, she didn't know that becoming a mom would mean her friendships would no longer exist.
Anastasiya: Homesick	Anastasiya just moved to a new state and she's missing her loved ones from back home. Her new neighbors are not as welcoming as her old ones. People do not smile in the grocery store, and no one invites her to any events. She misses the Chat and Chews with her girlfriends back home. She is in a new place and instead of feeling adventurous, she feels lonely.
Tracey: Life after Divorce	Tracey is recently divorced, and loneliness has a different meaning for her. For the first time in a long time, she is all by herself. Love doesn't reside in her home anymore and she's not sure how to start over. How is she going to show up to family functions and holiday staff parties alone? Who's going to fix the leaky toilet or change the light bulb in the hallway that she can't reach? Her bed went from warm to cold, as did her heart.
Jessica: The Strong One	Jessica seems to have it all together. She is known for being the strong one. Everyone comes to her for advice, comfort, and a shoulder to lean on. No one has ever seen her shed a tear, and she doesn't run to the vending machine to grab a Snickers when she's having

	a bad day. She's fierce and courageous. If a dude acts a fool even once, she'll block his number and move right on. No love lost from her perspective. Jessica is a rock. Or so everyone thinks. Because she is so solid, no one ever checks on her. No one ever thinks she needs them.
Shauna: Successful, but Single	Shauna is in her late thirties. She has a college degree, the career she's always wanted, her own house, car, tons of friends, no children, and yet, she's single. She's done everything she's ever wanted to do. Singleness has felt like a curse to her, and yep, she is lonely.

Ladies, at some point we all may have been, or may one day be, any of the women described in this chapter. I wanted you to meet these girls because I wanted you to see yourself in them. You may resonate with one more than another, or you may see yourself in a few of these women. I introduced you to them because many of us have the misconception that loneliness is all about our marital status.

Ladies, I am very much like Shauna. She is my story. I'm thirty-eight years old with my own house and car, and a master's degree. Ten years ago, I entered the career of my dreams. I am a Christian and an active member in my church where I volunteer and even hold a few leadership positions in ministry. I love bowling, playing kickball, and watching basketball. I'm someone who invests in my hobbies and spends time with family and friends. Game nights are life, and

I can even cook a little bit. Music soothes my soul, and dancing brings me absolute joy.

But then, why do I feel down sometimes? How does someone who does all these things feel so lonely? I am thirty-eight and I have ALWAYS been single. So, I'm sure you can imagine, I'm all too familiar with loneliness. "I'm so tired of being alone, I'm so tired of on-my-own." That's that Al Green for you. It's exactly how I feel!

My two college degrees hanging on the wall do not keep me warm at night. My manicured nails are nice to look at, but my left hand sure feels like it's missing something. I feel that void from my ring finger all the way up to my heart. Then it reaches my head which tells me...*you should have been married by now*. And with each passing day, and new gray hair, it gets harder and harder to accept my state of being alone, and my feelings of loneliness.

We deal with loneliness in all walks of life. No one is immune to it. The Merriam-Webster Dictionary defines loneliness as being without company or cut off from others. It means not frequented by others and feeling sad from being alone. It also indicates that it produces a feeling of bleakness or desolation. Whether you are married or single, divorced or widowed, with children or childless, have a full house or an empty nest, we have all experienced loneliness. From several dates in a week, no dates at all, a busy schedule, or a blank calendar, we all have something in common. We know exactly what it feels like to be alone. And oftentimes, when we are alone, we feel lonely.

We could be in a room filled with people and feel isolated from everyone. We could have a million followers on social media but those 'likes' don't keep us company. Maybe you have a loving husband or boyfriend, but he is too busy to spend quality time with you. Maybe he does spend time with you, and you don't even feel his presence. Whatever your story is at this current moment, we want to explore how you deal with feeling lonely at work, home, church, school, and in social settings.

REFLECTION:

Let us take a moment to reflect on what we've just read. Record your responses to the questions in the spaces below.

1. I, Keah, am a lot like Shauna. Which girl from this chapter reminds you of yourself the most?

2. What do you have in common with her? How did you feel when you saw yourself in this woman? Write out your description.

3. How do you ***currently*** deal with loneliness in different social settings?

Chapter 2
What is Loneliness?

As mentioned before, the dictionary defines loneliness as sadness because one has no friends or company. Another meaning stated that it's the quality of being unfrequented and remote, isolation. How would you define loneliness?

Try this: Set a timer for two minutes and write down words that come to mind when you think of the word loneliness.

Let me guess. Your list includes some of these words…

Sadness	Bored	Unattractive	Lost
Isolation	Hurt	Abandoned	Unaware
Depression	Shame	Separated	Missing
Unwanted	Solemn	Overlooked	Desolate
Unloved	Ignored	Misunderstood	Desperate
Emptiness	Embarrassing	Forgotten	Unworthy
Failure	Envy	Yearning	Insignificant

If you have any of these words written down…ME TOO!

Our list could go on. Do you notice what these words have in common? To me, they all seem negative. The overall tone and mood of all these words reminds me of darkness. Why does loneliness have such a negative connotation? It simply does not feel good to be lonely, does it? Loneliness feels like we are on a deserted island, in a world where the silence is so loud, it's painful to our ears. The emptiness we feel is disappointing and heartbreaking.

I want you to think about when you have company in your home. When you are expecting company, you might feel more comfortable and at ease about their visit. You've likely had time to prepare both internally and externally, right? You've had time to tidy up in preparation for the visit and everything is just about in place because this visit isn't catching you off guard. The feelings and thoughts associated with this visit may be overall positive because this was a welcomed guest for the most part. You at least had a say in this visit. If you didn't feel like being bothered, you at least had the opportunity to say, "Now isn't a good time."

But what happens when company shows up that did not call first? What about when an uninvited guest pops up that you weren't expecting? Those feelings might not be so positive. That guest is unwanted. You didn't know they were coming. You had something else going on and you feel like they just invaded your personal space. Not so positive, right?

Look at the words you listed about loneliness. We all know that loneliness is coming to visit at some point in our lives, but we don't always know when. The feelings with uninvited company tend to be negative, as do feelings related to loneliness. Who would choose to feel these things? I don't think anyone would on purpose, but the reality is that we are all going to experience these emotions and feelings.

If feeling lonely causes us to feel any or all the words mentioned, what does that look like in our lives? Since we feel those feelings, are we projecting loneliness? Since we are lonely, do people see sadness in our eyes? Can they tell that we may feel overlooked and ignored? Do they feel the hurt and pain behind our expressions? Does the tone of our voice sound desolate to anyone? What about our attitude? Is it a reflection of the sorrow that we feel? Are we walking around looking as lost and unworthy as we may feel?

We know it's inevitable to completely avoid loneliness, but isn't there a time limit for it? We won't experience it for too long, right? Eventually, when loneliness visits our lives, that thing must be gone at some point soon, right?

The irritation and burden of unwanted guests begins to wear on us. An unwanted guest is not always a person coming over to visit you. It's any circumstance that enters our lives. If it is unwanted, we likely feel afflicted by it. The weight of these emotions can be extremely heavy. As we feel these things, do we become them? We've heard of the saying, "You are what you eat," but we can also say, 'You are what you feel.' Since we feel that way, we're likely to walk in that way. I know I do. Think about our clothes. We use them to cover up. It's what people see when they see us. If you are lonely, and you feel miserable about it, it's more likely you'll walk around dressed in sadness because that's how you feel.

At times, loneliness has prompted me to dress myself in these negative emotions. I can look like them, I can sound like them, and I can act like them. Just like the clothes I put on every day, I put on words of sadness, hurt, hopelessness, and rejection. These words are what I used to cover myself. It's like they were a part of me. In fact, they felt like…me.

Just like unwanted house guests, loneliness has the potential to make us feel various negative emotions. Look at your list of words. Do they reflect your thoughts, words, and behaviors when you are feeling lonely? Why do you think you respond in this way? What images come up in your mind as you think about loneliness?

As we continue to explore our truths about loneliness, let's dig a little deeper about who we are and how these parts of us play a role in our response to loneliness.

REFLECTION:

What happens when you're feeling lonely? How do you think, speak, and behave when you're feeling this way?

Chapter 3
Pieces of Me

Part of my journey took me on a path where I had to figure myself out. By unpacking these parts, it helped me to see and understand who I am and why I behave and think the way I do. In sharing my experiences, I hope you will uncover the essence of your own character so that you can develop a keen understanding of who you are and how you relate to loneliness.

Like some of the experiences with 'The Ladies,' good friendships have also dwindled in my life. The silence in my house is extremely loud to me. I don't spend tons of time with my co-workers. When my students aren't with me, I'm in my classroom by myself, working alone with my door closed. Relaxing sounds from Pandora is all I hear while I work. I never find invitations to happy hours in my inbox either. I don't have any children. That biological clock ticks loudly in my mind, and it weighs heavily on my heart. It is incredibly disturbing and discouraging, and I often think about how my life is supposed to be different at this age.

These scenarios are my reality. I live this out every day, and I am sure many of you do too. But how does this really affect us? This may be just a book, but the examples are sometimes mirror images to our lives. We are lonely for many reasons, and it not only impacts how we feel, but it influences our choices.

I think I know myself inside and out. I know what I like, and what I don't like. I know what I need and don't need, what I want and don't want. After being in this body for thirty-eight years, I'm pretty familiar with myself. But I am still growing and changing within myself, and I had to engage in deep work, reflection, process, and change in order to continue learning about myself and my wants and needs. I had to dig deeper to reveal those pieces of me that caused me to react to loneliness in negative ways. I had to understand the parts that I am made up of in order to understand how I can respond differently when loneliness comes to visit. So, let me show you my process for how I discovered who Keah is and how Keah responds. I hope you, too, will engage in the work that is required for your own life's understanding.

Now, wait. This is not a conversation about having multiple personalities. This is more of a conversation about discovering who we are in order to understand what it is that we want and need in order to operate as our best selves. Sometimes, we as women are extremely serious; other times we may be super silly. Sometimes we are emotional, and there are moments when we could care less. There may be a conservative side and a side that likes to twerk in the mirror while listening to our favorite ratchet jam. Don't turn on "Da Butt" by E.U. around me - you will see a different side of Keah!

Here is what I did to explore more of my wants and needs, particularly when it came to dealing with loneliness. The picture below, shaped as puzzle pieces, helped me to identify parts of me that fit my roles in my family, friendships, profession, and personal life.

As you can see, I am a leader and educator who is strong and authoritative. I love prayer, devotion, meditation, reflection, and service. I want a hand to hold and a shoulder to lean on and I want to be that for others, too. I can be soft spoken. I must get recharged through stillness, adoring alone time and space to process. I also need to be active, whether it's watching the Golden Girls, playing kickball, listening to India Arie, or completing a Sudoku puzzle, I've got to do what makes me smile. My fears often try to take place throughout my parts, and I sometimes have the misconception that this part of me keeps me humble and cautious, but it mainly cripples me. I am a daughter, sister, niece, aunt, granddaughter, cousin, goddaughter, and godmother. I am also a friend, mentor, skilled teacher, and learner as well. Communication and affirmation are essential to me. I crave attention - and this is probably the piece that causes me to act out the most. But this is me – all me - and seeing this visual helped me to see myself.

As I identified each part, additional words were written to help me see things that are most important to me in those areas. We all have different parts of ourselves and although I feel pretty in tune with who I am, my parts can wear me out! And looking at this also begs the question: Since I know myself so well, why is the hardest relationship in life the one I have with myself?

Even with a keen awareness of ourselves, we can still enter into a web of deceptions, seclusion, and damaging behavior when we are not looking at something with the right perspective. But as promised, we'll see how this self-knowledge and awareness eventually helped me to see my loneliness through a different lens, and it will help you, too.

Learning about who we are can help us understand our beliefs and behaviors. As you uncover the different parts of who you are, I invite you to allow that discovery to help you reflect on the choices you've made and how you have responded to certain situations. You do not have to go through the same process I did to understand who I am, and what I want and need. Choose your own process. However, the most important thing is to take time to get to know you – in all your beautiful parts. Having this awareness about ourselves can ultimately lead to more positive outcomes in the way we handle loneliness.

REFLECTION:

You may use this puzzle placemat to identify your different parts, or you may choose to uncover, or discover, your parts in a different way. No matter the method, unpacking these things are critical to your changed perspective on loneliness.

PART II

COMPANY'S HERE:

UNDERSTANDING OUR

BEHAVIORS AND ACTIONS

Chapter 4
Lies and Negative Self-Talk

The Early Days

In the summer before I started high school, I began talking to a friend's cousin over the phone for a few weeks. We were excited that we'd be going to the same high school and would finally be able to see each other face to face. Decked in my fresh first day of school outfit, accompanied by a brand-new pair of gray New Balance tennis shoes, I was ready to meet my 'boyfriend.' But, when I approached him in the crowded, noisy cafeteria during lunch, he denied who he was. My heart sank. I could not believe he lied to me. I felt embarrassed, rejected, and dissed. My first day of high school was a nightmare.

When the liar's cousin called him on three-way with me later that day, she asked him why he lied. Not knowing I was on the phone, he said, "She's ugly." I was absolutely crushed, and it didn't help to have to see him passing in the hallways every day. I felt those words and they have been on repeat in my mind ever since. I can still hear those words twenty-four years later.

That was the beginning of my high school experience and things never got better for me during those tough years. I remained dateless and no one pursued me. No one asked about me and no one ever approached me. I didn't even have a date to my senior prom. I wore a pink, fluffy Cinderella dress, my hair was pinned up with spiral curls hanging down, and my cousin did a great job with my make-up. I felt beautiful, but my mind was consumed with thoughts of not even being worthy enough of a prom date. I looked like everything, but I felt like nothing.

Over the years, I experienced that same feeling of not being 'worthy enough' countless times. I had a crush on another guy all throughout middle school and high school, but we were only good friends. He was what I called my first bearded teddy bear. He made me feel respected and adored because we would talk all the time into the wee hours of the night. We kept in touch and hung out together through adulthood, and when we were about twenty-seven, I finally got the courage to ask him about us. He rejected me, saying, "I just don't see you that way," and shattered the hope I had held on to for years that we would be more than friends. Since we were so close, I always thought there was a possibility that one day he would see me as more, but he didn't. In fact, he told me that I would make some man really happy one day, it just wouldn't be him.

Since he only loved me as a friend, I believed that his rejection meant that I wasn't his type physically. In my mind, he found me unattractive and could never have an interest in me because I wasn't pretty enough. I wasn't his type. I wasn't anyone's type. That's what I thought because that's how I felt. This was the message I played over and over in my mind because of my early experiences. It became my story. My fictional story rooted in feelings, not truth.

Experiences like this had the potential to fuel my insecurities. Being lonely and feeling rejected has made me dwell in low self-esteem at times. The phrase may have been, "I'm not interested in you," or "I'm not ready for a committed relationship right now." But all I heard was, "You're ugly" and "You're unworthy." Believing those lies led me to damaging situations that I will discuss later.

Loneliness allowed me to believe lies and negative self-talk, making me think that the roles and positions I currently play in life are not important. At times, I have carried myself as if my worth were tied only to being a "girlfriend," "Mrs." and "mommy," and simply being Keah isn't good enough. I convinced myself that people didn't need me because my roles weren't significant. It is a battle as I go to war with my perceptions versus the actual truth.

Often derived from my past experiences, fears, brokenness, and insecurities, the lies I have fed myself were consumed so often, they began to seem real to me in my head, heart, and soul. These records were on repeat and played repeatedly. When I ate lies every day for breakfast, lunch, and dinner, I became full of that disgusting stuff! It was not nourishing my body at all, so I gave myself an opportunity for a diet change.

SLIGHTLY GROWING UP

I still sometimes struggle with the war on lies and negative self-talk in my life. Remember, like Shauna, I am single. I'm still single. And I have been trying to figure this thing out for a long time. I state my facts – I am smart, educated, spiritual, physically active, and emotionally connected, a lover, and a friend! Then, because I'm STILL single, the lies and negativity about singleness creep in, and my emotions and facts get all tangled up because of what I do not have in my life. It leads me to conclude that because I'm single, I'm unattractive, and my self-image and perception of my beauty contributes to my feelings about loneliness. This is how I've established that loneliness is a bad thing. This false assumption really affected me, but I'm so glad that the actual truth eventually has made its way into my heart.

Have you ever experienced any of this? I feel like I have been a constant contestant in the comparison game. I look at other women and think, '*She has someone who loves her and wants her, and she's so pretty. She's enough. She's better than enough. She's chosen.'* Even as a Christian, I don't always think God was talking to me when He said, "*I am fearfully and wonderfully made"* in Psalms 139:14 *(KJV)*. I'm not one of his wonderful works because no one wants me. Don't we all just want to be chosen? Whether it's by a man, for that promotion at work you've been wanting, the leadership role for the committee you're on, you just want to be noticed, right? Does anyone see us? Do we matter?

Romans 5:8 (NLT) says, "But God showed his great love for us by sending Christ to die for us while we were still sinners." I did not take this to mean that Jesus was the only one who wanted me. I yearned to be loved by others right here, right now! Wouldn't it be nice to be *invited* out somewhere by someone? The lines of communication work both ways, so why aren't *we* getting phone calls for play dates and brunch? Have you ever seen a post on social media to an event that you weren't invited to? Ouch!!! That hurts!

Sometimes my feelings of rejection lead me to wear a wardrobe of assumptions and lies. I literally felt like I had nothing else to put on each day. *Song of Solomon 4:7 (NLT) says "You are altogether beautiful, my darling, beautiful in every way."* I felt like that message didn't apply to dateless Keah. Where is the verse that says, "*You are unwanted because you're unattractive"?* That's the one I memorized.

Can you relate?

Whatever our situation is, we always want to be picked. We make ourselves known and available, so why won't someone select us already? Our resume looks good and we have expressed our interest, so pick us! Friends, this isn't just about getting picked for a relationship. It's about getting selected in general for things that we want the most – like kickball.

I have been playing kickball since 2013. It is one of my favorite hobbies, and it makes my entire heart smile. Now, I never said I was great at it. I just like it, and I truly wanted to get better. In the spring of 2018, I helped to start a women's kickball league. My team was amazing. I learned so much, and I felt like I had a cool bond with my teammates. The vibes were great, and we had a lot of fun together.

Then, I decided that I wanted an even bigger kickball fix, so I chose to play in two leagues for the upcoming fall season. I had my own team for the women's league with no problem, but in order to play in the co-ed league, I needed to join a team. This was harder than I thought. I didn't want to build or coach yet another team, I just wanted to link up with one.

One of the star athletes on my women's team said that she wouldn't be playing with us in the fall because she and her husband wanted to play in the co-ed league on a different night. I thought, 'Oh, cool, I could join their team!' This would be perfect, I thought, because I could play on

Wednesday nights and Friday nights. This was just what I needed to keep my schedule busy! Being busy helped me to escape the loneliness I so badly wanted to separate from.

Well, they didn't pick me. Even though I expressed several times that I was looking to be part of a co-ed team for the Wednesday night league, THEY DID NOT PICK ME. In fact, they picked a few other girls from our women's team, BUT NOT ME!

Girl, oh, girl did my feelings get triggered! I felt hurt, angry, betrayed, and rejected. The same feelings I experience in the dating world were now being felt because of kickball. It is incredibly hurtful to not be chosen. I would often feel like that lost and lonely kid at recess who no one chooses for their team. No matter what the reason is, it hurts.

Can you relate? Have you ever wanted something or to be a part of something, and you simply weren't picked? The reason why doesn't matter because the feelings will be the same. When we are not the chosen ones, we feel like we are less than anyone else. And because that's how we feel, sometimes, that's what we believe. The situation I experienced made me feel like I wasn't good enough to be on that co-ed kickball team, and now that lie had been planted inside of me. Without even realizing it, I started watering that thing. It was in me, inside me, growing. I connected it to other areas of my life, and it got so big that it overshadowed everything else. All reason and logic were gone. Forget about God's truth because that wasn't tangible for me. At times, I had been too faithless to see it anymore because I'd been blinded by the lies. Someone couldn't have missed a call because they were sleeping or just busy and hadn't had a chance to get back to me within my not-so-reasonable five-minute call back window. Oh, no! It meant that I was unworthy of the courtesy call back. I used the situations to draw negative conclusions about myself.

When someone did pay me compliments or give me positive feedback, it was foreign to me, so I rejected it. I learned the art of being dismissive. I couldn't accept compliments and words of affirmation although that's what I really wanted to hear. I shamed others for not loving me well enough even though I never even gave them the opportunity to love me. The lies already told me a secret - they'll fail you anyway, so guard your heart and don't let them get close.

Does this resonate with anyone? Is there a Belinda out there who's now retired, and she just can't see her value anymore? Now that your career is over, you just can't see how to start the next chapter? What about an Anastasiya? Because you've relocated, are you stuck in the house because you're too afraid that you'll be rejected? Are you paralyzed by fear of a community that you assume won't welcome you?

Natasha, you are married to a great man, but do you keep telling yourself that he's too busy for you? Do you feel he doesn't have time to spend with you because his work is his first priority? That he does all this for the family, so you can't nag him with another thing to do? Will holding you at night occupy too much of his precious time, so it's better that your needs are silenced? Would you be selfish if you asked for more of him? How dare you put more on his plate by asking for what you need! Are these some of the questions going through your mind?

Jessica, everyone thinks you have it all together. That's what it looks like. But did you just cover up your scent in some expensive perfume, girl? You may think they can't smell the funk that you feel, and maybe they can't. But you know it's there.

Ladies, what lies do you constantly tell yourself? About your life? About your circumstances? About your loneliness? What's the real reason you don't want company just showing up? Close your eyes and take three deep breaths. Now, count to ten slowly.

Keep reading my sisters. Do you know how we sometimes store bags inside of bags inside of bags inside of other bags? Have you ever purchased a luggage set with multiple compartments? That's what many of us have. Others may see the one big bag that we are carrying. But honey, we are about to unpack everything that's inside. We're taking it all out. We must shed light on the darkness in order to see our way to a positive shift in our mindset. Stay with me and let's keep going. Take another deep breath.

REFLECTION:

What are you feeling right now? Write them out here in this safe space. What are your thoughts? Whatever comes to mind for you right now, let it out. Don't silence her. Let her speak. Even if you don't believe her, let her voice be heard. Let the tears flow and let her have her say.

Chapter 5
Isolation

When I've asked people to share with me a word that comes to mind when they thought of loneliness, many shared the word isolation. Isolation is a state of being, so this is what we feel, or what we are in. But guess what? The word isolate is a verb.

It is an action, something we can do. It is a choice. Loneliness has not only caused me to feel isolated, but it has caused me to intentionally isolate from others. I have withdrawn and excluded myself from other people, including my family and close friends. That has been my response to loneliness. At times, that has been my choice.

You are probably wondering, *If I feel lonely, why would I purposely isolate myself from others?* Great question. I did this because I allowed loneliness to make me assume that others didn't want me around. Since I felt empty and overlooked, sometimes those feelings put me in an introverted state. Not necessarily because that's who I really am, but because I made a false assumption. I already felt rejected and unwanted, so I didn't even want to take the risk of trying to reach out to others. Do you find yourself doing the same thing?

My high school friends went away to college to prestigious universities. I went to a community college and didn't experience the campus life they did. They graduated on time and got jobs in their career field. I worked part time at a grocery store, struggling through my general courses. Since I dropped and failed many classes over the years, I really wasn't progressing in school, and I didn't feel like I measured up. I felt extremely behind in my life. People my age were getting married and starting families. I was dateless, and no one was even asking for my phone number. I was playing the comparison game again.

I isolated from others because I was jealous, resentful, injured, angry, confused, and scared. I didn't understand why my life was so different from everyone else's. I wanted relationships in my life, but I guarded my heart against them because I didn't think they'd be there for me anyway. How could my friends, who were now moms, leaders, and other roles, have time to be a friend to me? I felt like I had too many burdens and insecurities and no one's shoulder was strong enough for me to lean on. I would see things through a different lens eventually, but this was my struggle for a long time.

At one point, I found a bit of solace from these feelings of loneliness at church. When I was twenty-one, I left a big church to attend a smaller one where I felt I could meet more people and get involved. A close community, fellowship and involvement became huge desires for me. Not that this couldn't happen at larger churches, but something smaller was what I wanted.

I met a really good friend, and we began talking a lot and spending time together. I connected with this young lady because for one, we went to the same church, and two, she was single with no children. Just like me! It was easy for us to connect because we had the time and availability. We were very close for a while, and I was overjoyed to have a connection with someone like her. She was extremely intelligent, very caring, supportive, and she was intentional about being a good friend. She would ask me to stay at her house while she had to be out of town for work, she planned birthday celebrations for me, and we talked a lot.

But something changed between us, and things were never the same again. She started dating a guy from our church, and I felt like he took her time and her heart away from me. She no longer had time for our golden girl friendship because she was nurturing a relationship with her boo thang. And while I was happy that she found love with a remarkable guy, my jealousy and assumptions pulled me away from her. She didn't push me away, I pulled away. There is a huge difference between pushing and pulling. I chose to isolate myself from her because that was my way of protecting my heart.

My friend married her prince charming and they started a family. I didn't think she could balance being a wife, a mom, and my friend. I didn't give her a chance to see if she could or not, and I rolled out on my own. I missed her friendship dearly for years because my thought was that we no longer related to each other. She's a wife, I'm not. She's a mom, I'm not. She had advanced in her life, and I felt like I had stood still. Our lives were too different, and she just would not have the time.

My truth is that although I may be lonely and want friendship and company, I sometimes feel that I cannot make the effort anymore. I fear someone's answer will be no, so I don't even ask. I wasn't good with accepting no. Without even understanding their no, I automatically took it personally, and the rejection would creep in. I am so glad for the change in heart that ultimately occurred. It takes intention and growth, but things soon change.

As I withdrew in relationships, social settings, church, and even at work, I convinced myself that isolation seemed like the only solution to dealing with the burdensome feelings I so often experienced. It's a very conflicting place to be in because while I long for connection, attention, and love, I don't know how to receive it. But stay tuned. I learned that this haven isn't so safe after all. We can either stay in the bondage that isolation brings, or we can venture out to enjoy meaningful and healthy experiences with others, including ourselves.

Reflection:

Describe how isolating from others has impacted you. How did you feel? What did you gain from isolating from others? What have you learned?

Chapter 6
Toxic Behavior

What comes to mind when you think of the word toxic? I immediately think of something bad that we are not supposed to have. I think of something that is not good or healthy for us. Many people think of toxic as being synonymous with poison, something that is deadly, hazardous, and dangerous. Some view it as something that is dysfunctional, overwhelming, draining, and sickening.

There could be toxic people in our lives, or toxic thoughts, activities we engage in, foods we consume, habits we have, and feelings we encounter. Whatever toxic behavior is present in your life, think about its root. Where did it come from? What does it do for you? What does it do to you?

It is time to unveil our toxic behaviors. And to help you with this, I'm going to share several of my experiences. Yes. I am going to reveal some of my most personal experiences with you. Why? To show you that you are not alone. To show you that it is not just about intimacy. This is part of the work that happens when you want to get out of negative thinking and behaviors because of loneliness. Again, you are not alone. Ready? Jump!

Here's to Our Health!

For years, I have been a borderline diabetic. Already diagnosed with high blood pressure and high cholesterol, I was supposed to be careful. I was supposed to lose weight, exercise, and cut down on my carb intake so I wouldn't have to go on medicine. I didn't want that for my life. I didn't want to be on a bunch of medication and I certainly didn't want to have diabetes. Not me! Can I tell you what I really thought? I thought, "I'm not even that big." What a true misconception I had about the whole diabetic concept!

After a few gym memberships and failed commitments to walk daily, I had not lost any weight. My numbers were increasing and in June of 2018, I was classified as a diabetic. I was put on medication until I could control my sugar on my own by losing weight. I was ashamed of myself and I was scared.

I knew that losing weight wouldn't be easy for me because I'm an emotional eater. Loneliness makes me feel so empty and food is my remedy. Sweet, starchy, carb filled food makes me feel full, and to give that up is simply uncomfortable. Not only do I choose to eat a lot of the wrong foods, but I also overindulge. Sometimes I'm not even hungry; I just eat because it's available.

Eating out is a treat to myself at the end of a stressful day. I'm a teacher, so I have a lot of stressful days. Grabbing a bite to eat on the drive home seems like a reward for being overwhelmed, overworked, tired, and underappreciated. With plenty of food already in the house, I just want to feel full to relieve myself of feeling empty.

A Little Retail Therapy, Anyone?

You know what else is toxic for me? Spending money! I can't turn my back on a good sale. When I see an amazing bargain,

I feel like God opened the windows of heaven and said, "Keah, I put this here just for you to buy." I feel like it is His gift to me. Even if it's something I don't need or want for myself, I'll buy it for someone anyway. Sometimes I'll buy something, and I'll have no idea who it's for. I will find someone to give it to later, but I just can't resist a good sale. That would be retail idiocy.

Retail is therapy and it takes my mind off feeling lonely. It's a temporary distraction and it helps me to escape my desolate thoughts. But there is a big problem – I usually can't afford to buy half of what I purchase!

My shopping addictions are toxic because it has led me to a substantial amount of debt. If I get my mind on something that I really want, whether I need it or not, I just cannot rest until I get it. If I see something on clearance that is cute and is close to my size, I'll get it. Yep, for the right price, I will even buy stuff that I can't even fit. I'll convince myself that I'm being optimistic, and this will be my motivation to lose weight. Again, another toxic thought that leads to toxic behavior.

Let's Pause and Reflect

My sisters, there is a lot of toxic behavior we can get into. Things like drinking, gambling, lying, competing with others, watching certain things, gossiping, or listening to something. What is your 'thing'? When you are at your worst, what's your go to? Whether it is an enormous bowl of ice cream or a booty call to ol' unfaithful, most of us have something we cling to for comfort. And sweetie, there's no judgment here. Trust me.

Engaging in toxic behavior is my personal experience and loneliness has led me here, especially in the arms of the wrong men. You read earlier that I have always been single. But that does not mean I haven't been in 'situation-ships'. I can't fault myself for trying to find love. The problem is that even when I knew love wasn't there, I still stayed. I still engaged, held on, and tried. That is toxic.

Although loneliness caused me to isolate from others such as my family and friends, it did not cause me to isolate from men. Instead of keeping me away from men, it pushed me towards men – the wrong men. I exhibited toxic behaviors in these relationships.

Men, Men, Men, Men!

I have always been extremely addicted to male attention. Perhaps it is because I didn't receive a lot of attention from my dad. I grew up with my mom, and although I saw my dad, we weren't as close as I needed us to be. I have tried to fill that void from other men in my life. Not that they could replace my dad, but that validation from a male that loves and adores me was missing. There was a hole in my heart because of that substantial absence.

I have been bluntly rejected by men and I still tried to pursue them hard. I thought if I just show him how nice and loyal I am, he'll really see me. If I just show him how determined and steadfast I can be, he'll be like, "Wow!" and he'll pick me.

When I was twenty-five, I reconnected with someone and by this time, he had it going on. He showed interest in me real quick and I was hooked. I remember our first date when he took me to see the movie, *Transformers.* Sitting next to him, I felt like I was on top of the world. He was a tall, thick, bearded teddy bear with dimples. He had the most beautiful hairy legs and was incredibly built. Hugging him took my breath away, and his kisses…whew!

We were both working and still going to school. But the difference was that I had all the time in the world to give to him, and he gave me none. After the first few weeks of talking, he was completely unavailable. He made himself accessible physically from time to time when he was in need, but other than that, he was a ghost. I hated that. But the more distant he was, the harder I tried. I made every effort and attempt in the world for him to pay attention to me and to love me.

He always said that his life revolved around school and I really thought that once he graduated, he would have more time for us. I held on tightly and persisted because I was sure that he'd finally choose me once he had more time. He didn't. As soon as he graduated, he married someone else. I wasn't even aware that he was dating anyone else. SMH. There went my happy ending with him.

To keep from being completely alone all the time, I recycled men I should have shredded. I couldn't block those numbers or delete them from my memory because I needed them just in case. When I felt lonely, I needed a temporary fix. It was not always sex, ladies. Sometimes it was just for attention or compliments. We just want to hear a Barry White voice even if he is playing broken records. It's better than hearing silence, right? At least that is the lie I told myself. The feeling of being wanted and loved really affected my interactions with men.

I remember when I said good-bye to my maternal grandmother. My world wasn't clear. I was not ready to lose her, and I was a bit numb. There was a hole in my heart, and I felt lost. I needed and wanted her here with me. Not only was there a huge void from her not being here, but I also felt incredibly alone. This is where I wanted a man to console me while I grieved the loss of my grandmother. I was supposed to be in a big man's bear hug as he comforted me in his warm embrace. I should have been able to smell his cologne as I rested my head on his shoulder. He was supposed to hold me while I cried myself to sleep at night. He was supposed to be sitting right beside me at her funeral and my hands were supposed to be wrapped in his as tears fell from my face. He was supposed to bring me meals in bed to make sure I was eating. He was supposed to be there for me during this time of grieving. But instead, I was mourning two people, my grandmother and him. Neither of them was there.

So, I got proactive and decided to do something about it. That same month, I came across a profile on eharmony. I was smitten. This gentleman's profile from New Jersey had caught my attention. He was my complete type, another tall bearded, teddy bear, and everything on his profile was music to my ears.

I couldn't believe that I was experiencing such a blissful feeling from someone I had never even met in person. But girlfriend that was short lived. After a few weeks, I couldn't reach him. So, what did I do? I did what only a sensible woman would do. I called hospitals and jails. I called the rental office to the apartment complex where he lived, and I called his cell phone carrier to see if there was any activity on his phone. I panicked at the thought of losing something that seemed like true potential, so I just could not sit still.

After a while, Mr. MIA answered the phone again. He shared that he had completely shut down because of what he had been going through. He was having a great deal of financial trouble and he was about to lose his truck. So, what did I do? You know I sent 'my man' some money. Nope, he hadn't declared that he was my boyfriend, but I felt like he was going to be, so I had to help a brotha out! If I poured into him, he would pour into me, and I was oh so thirsty! Notice the toxic behavior illustrated here? I had not even met the man in person, so this was not about sex. Here was a man who was clearly broken from whatever was going on in his life, and I ignored the red flags. Yes, we all experience hardships, but it wasn't wise of me to think he was capable of pursuing and nurturing a relationship while he was going through his own challenges.

For months, he went in and out. To my knowledge, he began to lose everything. His apartment, his vehicle, his cell phone, and didn't seem to have a pot to piss in.

He would call when he could. I sent him money a total of maybe six times, and I just felt bad for him. I believed his story, and I just felt compelled to help this man get back on his feet. I could tell how depressed he was. Being a man and not being able to provide for himself, or his children, and having to ask his woman who's not really his woman for money - it just ate him up. Poor him!

He finally agreed to let me come to New Jersey. With an overnight bag packed, I drove up there wearing a pretty blue and white maxi dress. I had dark purple polish on my toes and my hair was out with loose curls despite the August heat. I finally got to see him for the first time around five o'clock that evening, and he was real. He was the handsome man in the pictures. A tall, muscular, teddy bear with a thick beard wrapped me in his big arms and he was real. I could not believe it. Although I breathed a sigh of relief, I was beyond confused when he told me he couldn't stay. He said he got called into work and would try to get back to me as soon as he could. *Wait, what? I just drove a few hours to see you and spend time with you, rented a room for us to stay in, and you're going to leave?????*

He apologized and assured me he would be back as soon as he could. We talked for about two hours and then he said he'd be back soon. I walked him to the company van he was driving, we hugged, he said, "I'll be right back." He looked me in the eyes and said, "I'll be right back, Babe." Out of his mouth, he said, "I'll be right back." With his lips moving and sound coming out, I heard, "I'll be right back."

I never saw or heard from him again. I was in New Jersey by myself to visit him, and he left, and never came back. I was up all night. The next morning, I drove around looking for him for about an hour, and with no real leads, there was nothing else I could do but go home. I cried on the entire drive back.

That wasn't the last time something like that happened. In February of 2019, I had met another really sweet, bearded teddy bear for my birthday weekend while visiting the Virginia Beach area. We were introduced and I was infatuated. He showed me time, attention, and intentionality that I had never experienced before. Although he told me that he didn't have the capacity to pursue a relationship due to things he was dealing with in his life, my hopes were high. He said that he could see this really being something, and he really liked the vibe. I took that and planned our wedding in my head. I was so fueled by our attraction to one another and by the fact that he was showing so much interest in me, I really did not hear him. His attentiveness alone was something so brand new to me, and I was excited about the potential of us. I hadn't been that close before. I had just been the convenient booty call before, but he seemed to want something different from me. I thought, "Wow, Happy Birthday to me!"

When I got home, I thought things would be on and poppin'. I thought we would continue to talk and text in abundance and send each other mushy emojis and gifs throughout the day. We lived three hours apart, but we discussed that we were going to get to know one another. Virginia Beach is my home away from home anyway, so the distance wasn't going to be a problem.

The distance wasn't the issue, but his slow pace accelerated mine and I acted like a complete fool. I called and called a lot. I texted even more. The closer I stepped toward him, the further he backed off. I was rushing and pushing, and he got turned off and irritated.

I tried to relax a little bit. I didn't text or call as much, and I thought I'd show him that I could calm down and stop being so 'pressed'. I quieted myself down by going back to counseling and I began to fast. Not specifically for him, but because I wanted to calm my anxieties. I realized this pattern was all too familiar and I kept repeating the same aggressive behavior when getting to know someone. This was not cute, and I needed to change. I did not want to lose him.

I knew I'd be visiting the Virginia Beach area towards the end of March and I was certain that we'd reconnect, and the spark would reignite. Despite us not being in touch often, I just knew we'd see each other and realize the chemistry hadn't faded. After two weeks of no communication because I had put myself in 'time out' and I was trying to prove that I could give him space, when I got to Virginia Beach, I texted...

"Hey, I'm in town. Can I see you?

I'm at a rehearsal.

Will you be free later?

It depends on what time I get out of here. I doubt it."

He didn't say, "Hey, how are you? You're here for the weekend? Oh cool, I'd love to see you. I'm busy this evening, but we can definitely connect this weekend." Nothing of the sort! He was cold, stand-offish, and distant.

I wasn't in town specifically for him, but I definitely expected to spend time with him again. I had gotten my makeup done at the Mac counter. I had even purchased products that I really couldn't afford just so I could look pretty for him that weekend. I had gotten a manicure and pedicure, so my nails were polished a pretty shade of purple. I had gone to the hairdresser and gotten my hair dyed a gorgeous shade of red and I wore it with loose curls. I had on a cute black dress with black boots. I hardly ever wear dresses. The last time I saw him, I was in sweatpants with my hair natural all over my head. But he liked me then and he held me, and he saw me. He held my hands, looked into my eyes, and kissed me so softly. A month later, I got all dolled up, and he didn't even want to see me. I didn't matter to him anymore.

Did I give up? Nope! I called and texted continuously all weekend. I was determined to be face to face with him to SEE if he was still interested. His actions had already shown me he wasn't, but I had to SEE it up close. I had to HEAR it directly from him. Hints do nothing for me. I had to actually hear it from his mouth with my ears. I had to accept the truth that was staring me right in the face. I didn't see him or talk to him that weekend.

Lessons Learned

Sisters, there is nothing in the world wrong with you or me wanting companionship. There's nothing toxic about wanting to spend your life with someone. We often recognize when something isn't right for us, and what do we do with it? For me, I kept on pressing. I kept trying. Yes, a girl who longed to be pursued had become the ultimate chaser.

Have you ever wanted something so badly that you can't even still yourself to really receive it? You can't even be calm enough to watch and wait as it embraces you? Instead, you chase, and you hunt too hard. Too aggressively. You hold it so firmly that it feels suffocated by you, so it leaves you because your grip is too tight. Has this happened to you?

This is my truth. From twenty years ago, every year since then, I am that girl who doesn't know how to rest when it comes to men. I don't know how to chill out. When someone comes into my life, in my head, he sweeps me off my feet very quickly, and I imagine our wedding and name our children. I envision his proposal when all he said was, “Hello.”

While the dream can be beautiful and filled with hope, it can also be toxic if it’s not managed well. For me, my lack of patience, understanding, space, and peace has been hazardous. It has been what has caused many possibilities to come to an abrupt halt. My insecurities and belief in lies and negative self-talk have made me uneasy and very hard to deal with. Yes, I met some no-good dogs along the way, but many others were great guys who I just tried to control out of my own insecurities. I needed and wanted to feel liked. And because of this, I pushed.

Without even knowing it, I made guys responsible for my happiness, and the lack of it. I put it on them to fill me up because life had left me so empty and broken. They were supposed to take all those shredded pieces and mend them back together and quickly!

My toxic behavior was repetitive. Although I was aware of the damage my actions were causing, I couldn’t stop. I repeated the same patterns over and over again, and I fell on my face each time. Although I’d have a major revelation and journal about my errors, when the time came around again, I engaged in the same toxic behavior that I knew by heart.

My excuse for engaging in these behaviors was loneliness. I showed up dressed as her and I introduced myself as her. My actions and attitude literally said, “Hi, my name is Loneliness.” I hung with her and although she was my worst enemy, I made her my company. She was the unwanted, uninvited guest in my life, but I opened the door for her each time. When people wondered where I was, she was my alibi.

I wore her brand of clothes and perfume. I consumed her for breakfast, lunch, and dinner. When I spoke, I talked in her language and when I listened, I only heard her grim voice. I became her and she overshadowed me. No one could see me because Loneliness was bigger.

Although I didn't really like her, Loneliness was with me. In my head, my heart, and my soul. She had control over my mind. She sang to me and I danced a dismal dance with her. She shattered my dreams and stole my joy. She robbed me of hope and confined me to bondage. Her ruthlessness held me captive and she moved me to toxicity. But she had a secret for me. When she showed up as my company, she came bearing gifts. She wasn't out to punish me after all.

I've shared with you how I have responded and sometimes still respond to loneliness. When I've felt lonely, I've clothed myself in its negative aspects. My wardrobe of lies, isolation, and toxic behavior has been damaging for me. It was important for me to own my truth so that I can begin to heal. I wanted to uncover all of this so that I no longer carry it with me. Now, I get to choose a new wardrobe. Now, I get to respond to my company in a different manner.

Whatever negative things loneliness has led to in your life, I hope that you feel comfortable enough to release it. We're on this journey together to find the safe space to lay down the burdens we've been carrying. Releasing our baggage here will allow us to travel lighter for the next part of our remarkable journey.

I gave you a very detailed, intimate picture of how loneliness has affected me to show how it can have a negative impact on how we think and behave but get ready for some good news. I am so encouraged by the fact that I know a God who is bigger than the lies and negative self-talk I've spoken to myself! He's greater than the isolation I engrossed myself in, and He's stronger than the toxic behavior I engaged in. He has a new wardrobe available for me and I'm delighted to change my clothes. I can respond to the company of loneliness in a new way because He's prepared me for her visit.

To all the Samantha's, Victoria's, Natasha's, Belinda's, LaShay's, Mariana's, Anastasiya's, Tracey's, Jessica's, and Shauna's out there, there is another side to loneliness that can be dealt with in a healthy and positive way. Loneliness doesn't only produce negativity, darkness, and oppression. There can be light at the end of the tunnel, and I'm blessed to say that sometimes, I experience it. If you have not seen the brighter side of loneliness yet, just know that you can. Light isn't just at the end of the tunnel. We don't have to get to the finish line to see the light. Light is along the way and I really believe it's shining for us.

The personal development work I participated in with my REAL Women Rock sisters, a group who empowers women to be their best internal and external selves, ushered me into learning how to accept and love each piece of me. This safe space allowed me the opportunity to get to know myself and uncover the essence of Keah so that I could walk in wholeness and truth, no longer living in brokenness and bondage. This work has led me into a healthy relationship with myself and because of my new commitment to Keah, I am able to change my wardrobe, jam to a new playlist, and see loneliness from a different perspective.

It's my pleasure to usher you into a similar space. Regardless of what season you're in, you too can be your authentic self, loving each part of who you are, and walking in wholeness and freedom. The choices we've made and the circumstances we've faced don't have to shame us. We can reshape our own stories which begin with embracing our truths to uncover who we really are and how we need to move in order to be whole and free.

Your process may look different from mine. But the important part is to get to know who you are. As you uncover who you are, this work will help you to understand your own behaviors, patterns, and reactions to life's circumstances. You will learn how to give yourself what you need once you truly discover what it is that you want. For me, I discovered that the very thing I was lonely for was…me.

REFLECTION:

Take a few deep breaths. Breathe in deeply and when you push the air out, be sure to make a sound with it. I want you to identify the toxic behaviors you've engaged in. The purpose isn't to shame yourself. This is a guilt-free, judgment-free zone. The goal is for you to unpack it by stating it and getting free. Call it out so that it can be released. The only way from here…is up.

PART III

BE MY GUEST:

A NEW PERSPECTIVE

SSSHHHHH!!!!!

Since I've spent every moment for the past three weeks thinking of the perfect words to say, I'm ready to be heard. I've rehearsed it over and over a million times, so let the conversation begin. The one where I say I'm sorry, and I mean it, but I'm really trying to speed up your forgiveness. Let me spit the verse that forces you into immediate action because we don't have time to waste.

I'm sorry. I was impatient, but I still need you to hurry up because my anxiety isn't built for waiting and enduring the process. I can't focus on the journey because I only want the destination, and I have just the right lines to get us on that fast track.

I want your actions to match your words but let me write the script with stage directions for you. I already designed your costume as well, and I've envisioned the perfect plot. So, let's press play on this production, directed by me.

I want you to lead and take the initiative, but I'll give you the instructions to the manual of me. I'll leave nothing for you to wonder about, and you won't even have to chase. I've been praying for a beautiful surprise, but I've already planned it for myself. I just need you to show up, but I'll be the host.

Since I already know the lyrics to the song I want to dance to, I can't vibe to anything unfamiliar. Your version is slightly off. Maybe it's in a different key, or to a different beat, so I just can't relax in the groove. Your rendition isn't as fast as mine, and it makes me uncomfortable and restless because I really, really want to finally dance.

I don't have peace because I don't know that tune. The flow is different from what I have played in my head all these years. Is this the remix because it's different from what I ordered?

Since it isn't music to my ears, I'll stop listening completely. I'll try desperately to get the track I want back, and I'll get so caught up in the controls, I won't hear clearly. I'll sing the way I want the music to play as if my commands will give it life again, and I'm hoping you'll catch on to the melody of my song. I want you to match my exact sound. But the only voice I hear is mine, so I'll start singing louder. I'll get exhausted and then it won't even be music to my ears either.

Hopefully, something in me will say, "Shhhhhh". Then I'll start listening instead. No longer singing, just listening.

Prayerfully I'll resign as the director and as the DJ. And then, as I just listen, I will realize I can rock to a new sound. One that I didn't compose. And as it turns out, I'll find that I can dance to that song too.

Wake Her Up

TGIF, but not really. This means I have to face Friday night. And then comes Saturday, followed by Sunday. I should be happy, but things get really quiet on the weekends. It's usually so quiet, the silence is deafening. I can't stand it.

If nothing's on the agenda, Loneliness is gonna come and torment me again. I can't stand her, and I don't wanna face her. It's been a long week, and the last thing I wanna do is have to battle with her.

She makes me reach for the phone that I wish would ring with a call or ding with a message. When it doesn't, I reach for it in search of something, anything. That's when I begin to play old songs and reruns of episodes I've seen before. That's no fun because they don't make me smile. I was the star of the show and the ending wasn't good. No, I don't wanna watch that again. But I need something to do.

It's the weekend, and it makes me weak. It prompts me to scroll through social media as I focus on the status I wish I could post about my reality. Since I have no cool updates to share, I'll roll my eyes at the joy everyone else is experiencing that should be mine.

Since I have no plans, I'll just get full some other way. Junk food and carbs will be my company since no one else is near. Maybe I'll stay at work late pretending to be productive. No one has to really know I'm too afraid to go home. There's an uninvited intruder in my house and her name is Loneliness. She's unwelcomed in my life, but she shows up anyway.

I don't have anything to do so how about I go shopping? I can front like there's money in my wallet and become outraged when my card is declined. I can act like it's someone else's fault and shame them for inconveniencing me. I'll pretend to call the bank first thing on Monday morning.

It's the weekend, and Loneliness is torture. She imposes on me and forces me to sit in my sorrow. So I sit. I cry. I complain. I try to find a solution, but my way never works. Then I give up, and I try to sleep. But she must have something against resting because she wakes her up every time.

After the tears have fallen and my eyes are swollen, the failed attempts to fixing it my way, digging through the past, and the agony of trying to fight her the best way I know how, she wakes her up.

Loneliness reminds all of me that there's a part in me who's asleep, and she challenges me to bring her as a guest to my pity party. "Wake her up", she says. "You often forget to invite her, but it's not too late".

When Loneliness gets really loud, as loud as she can get, other parts of me wake up. When these parts awaken, Loneliness has no choice but to retreat. As she makes her exit, she looks back with a smirk on her face as if to say, "I thought so", and then she's gone. Knowing she achieved what she came to do, she's gone when she wakes her up.

Chapter 7
Revelation

You've read a shortened version of some of the countless stories I have about my damaging behavior in chapter six. While I feel like it can absolutely suck to be alone, there have been valuable lessons from every hurtful experience. I've experienced many disappointments that left me heartbroken, but I now realize that I can't expect the people who wounded me to be the ones to heal me. I always thought that having reasons for their actions may have helped me sleep better at night, but at the end of the day, I must take responsibility for my healing. I also must acknowledge my role in every experience as well because I certainly played a part.

For every unanswered phone call, unreturned text message, and every single ounce of rejection I've ever experienced, although it hurts, I embrace the lesson now. Companionship would be awesome, but how many of us have been in someone's presence and still felt very much alone? Doesn't a relationship produce a fullness? Then why is it that we often still feel empty? For me, I had to accept the fact that I was simply looking to be 'un-lonely.' Having a significant other, plenty of friends to hang out with, gatherings, and events to attend consistently allows me to feel 'un-lonely.' Feeling lonely is uncomfortable. But sometimes simply putting a bandage over a wound doesn't heal it. It simply covers it up.

Instead of wishing the loneliness away, I had to allow myself to feel it. I had to address the trauma of each negative experience and take a deeper look into the situation that impacted my behavior, thoughts, and feelings. My complete adult life had consisted of chasing men. Although I knew I didn't have to chase what was meant for me, I couldn't help it. Fear drove me to chase others and the girl that wanted nothing more than to be pursued, took on the pursuit. It was time for me to figure out why. I had to get to the root of my issues so that I didn't continue to plant the same seeds again and again.

Instead of shaming that persistent part of me, I needed to listen to and understand this part of me. I validated her feelings and apologized for acting out in such toxic ways. That courageous conversation I had with myself and God led to an amendment. I had to embrace forgiving myself, stop playing the victim, and decide how to respond to loneliness in a healthy way.

Shifting my mindset and attitude is truly a process, and please know, I don't always get it right. But God's grace is so very real. Once I stopped looking to others to heal what felt broken in me, I started to change. My circumstance or situation didn't necessarily change, but I changed. I was left with an appreciation for the disappointments that came in the form of rejection. A revelation took place, and because of it, a shift in my mindset took place as well. I saw the glass as half full, instead of half empty.

Google's English dictionary defines a revelation as a surprising and previously unknown fact, especially one that is made known in a dramatic way. All of my encounters and battles with loneliness have seemed dramatic to me. Loneliness was a guest that I never wanted to see. She's definitely an unwelcomed presence in my life, but wanted or not, she's going to show up and I have power over how I respond to her visit.

We know that we experience loneliness for various reasons, and I want you to know that I'm sensitive to your experience. For you, it may not be about relationships. Although that is much of my story, I want to reiterate that loneliness occurs for many reasons. We have all experienced some type of rejection or hurt that left us feeling lonely. And didn't you just want to hurry up and feel better and be over it? I like using the analogy of traveling or getting somewhere. We often just want to rush to the endpoint to get to the desired outcome. We're so focused on the destination, we often neglect the journey.

TEACHABLE MOMENT

I'm going to put on my teacher hat for a moment and bring you with me into my classroom. As an elementary school teacher, I teach students about the elements of a story. Let's think of our circumstances like a story. Each story has a plot which consists of a beginning, middle, and end. In the beginning, the problem is introduced. The middle consists of the process of solving the problem. The solution comes at the end when typically, a theme or message is revealed to the main character. There's always a lesson to be learned, right?

Let's put this idea into the context of a situation we may face. You have an experience, and some sort of problem arises. Challenges and adversity do not make us feel good. Not saying we can't handle them, but we usually just can't wait for it to be over. Connect this to an unwanted visitor. Imagine a guest that you just cannot wait to leave. So, you'd rather jump straight to the ending, the solution. They're gone, it's over, you feel relieved, the end.

Let me put this into the context of something I've recently faced. Loneliness is at my doorstep again banging to enter. Her unwelcomed visit causes a great deal of stress, anxiety, and irritation. Yet another guy has rejected me and how long is it going to take for me to just get over him? Can't I just forget about him already, so it doesn't hurt anymore? Can't I just be swept off my feet by someone else, so I don't have to be sad anymore? Can't I just skip right to the end of this chapter where things are solved, and everything is better? Can we just fast forward to my happily ever after?

If I jump straight to the end of this story, what am I missing? The middle! Remember the middle is the bulk and grit of a story. It's the process. Often in our loneliness, we just want to jump straight to the end when we feel 'un-lonely' so that we don't have to feel the discomfort of the process. That's where the pain is. That's where the work is. But that's also where the healing takes place when we endure the process. We cannot experience restoration, rehabilitation, and recovery without the process in the middle.

YOUR CONNECTIONS

On your journey, what are some things that have caused you to experience loneliness? Whether you decide to make note of those situations in a journal or in the pages of this book, I encourage you to take the time to reflect on what has led you to feel lonely. Again, it doesn't usually feel good. Not only is there a very real void from the lack of company, but it typically does something to our mind and spirit. We won't deny the realistic pain we may feel and the disappointment that seems to envelope us. We won't put a bandage on it and wear the mask and pretend it doesn't bother us. We're not going to say, "I'm just gonna be a big girl." We're going to be honest and acknowledge the truth that the middle part is hard.

We can show our scars and be candid about how they got there. We can cry it out and not feel ashamed about our tears. Let's stop hiding our tears and apologizing for crying. Somewhere along the way, many of us have learned to stuff our tears because we think it makes us look weak and it makes others uncomfortable. We don't want to inconvenience others, so we stop the tear flow, but what does that do? That stuff stays trapped inside us. And because it doesn't come out, we deny ourselves the opportunity to allow our tears to be cleansing and usher us into our healing. Easily, we get comfortable in dysfunction because that's what we're used to. When we don't release it, it carries over to the next situation and then we're stuck in a vicious cycle because we haven't healed.

TEARS

When a child is crying, after you asked what happened, what's the next thing you say? When I was a little girl, I know I was surrounded by people who loved me. But when I cried, they always said, "Don't cry." Perhaps that's just an average comforting phrase that just casually comes out, but have you ever thought about what it means? I'm guilty of it too because that's the first thing I say to my students when they're crying at school. "Awww, don't cry." I think it's just a natural response.

We don't want to see anyone hurt, upset, or crying. It's just odd for us to sit there and watch somebody cry. It seems kind of rude, doesn't it? I don't think my parents realized the healing that could have potentially taken place if they would have just let me cry. No one in my family is very affectionate, so perhaps it was uncomfortable for them. Maybe my mom just wanted me to be strong because that's how she had to be as a single parent. Maybe it was generational. Her mother didn't let her cry either so maybe she just didn't understand how it worked to be comforting. Like many mothers, maybe she thought that telling me not to cry was in fact comforting.

But guess what? Stuffing those tears was toxic for me. Because I was always shielded from hurt and pain, I rushed to get out of it so I wouldn't have to feel it. I rushed to the destination and missed out on everything that had to be learned and endured in the process of the journey. I tried to shield myself from it as an adult. I didn't let myself cry, so when I felt hurt, rejected, betrayed, or lonely, I worked hard to numb the pain instead of crying through it. I tried to rush right through the middle of my stories in a race to get to the end where I'd feel better. I couldn't run to my parents or to anyone in my family because no one dealt with emotional stuff. Everyone just told me to be a big girl and stop crying. So that's what I tried to do.

The same pattern continues as an adult. When I lost my dad four years ago, people would pat me on the shoulder and say, "Don't cry." As my mom's health declined, everyone said, "Don't cry." I'm not looking for words or answers. I'm just looking for a safe space to grieve out loud in the middle of my story. Many of us are in the middle of a situation and we just need a safe place. Grieving privately in the darkness has made us feel like there's something wrong or unnatural about our hurts. We just need the freedom to be able to process them out loud in the right way. Because we haven't, it's been translated in unhealthy ways that didn't allow us to truly heal.

The same is true for affection and attention. I lacked affection growing up because my family just isn't wired that way. I longed for hugs and cuddles and that only intensified as I got older. I thrive on positive praise and words of affirmation, but again, my family doesn't express themselves that way. So, when I got older, I found ways to get what I longed for. When we have needs that are never met, we sometimes find ways to cope however we can.

This reminds me of my students. They absolutely thrive on positive feedback. Whether it's a sticker on their paper, a verbal compliment, or a high-five, any type of positive recognition fuels them. It fills them up and allows them to feel a sense of accomplishment. For some, it provides clarity, reassurance, acknowledgment and simply says, "I see you." Don't we all just want to be seen?

Those simple words have so much power, and children aren't the only ones who need that type of affirmation. We all long for it. But for some of us, perhaps something or someone made us feel needy or thirsty for needing to be recognized. Maybe we felt like attention seeking was a bad thing and therefore, we stopped asking for what we needed. It's even possible, we started seeking from the wrong sources, for the wrong reasons. That's because our needs never changed.

Once I realized what I lacked as a child growing up in terms of affection, attention and emotional availability, I had a decision to make. I could remain the victim of unfortunate circumstances and blame my upbringing, or I could reflect and respond in a healthy way. So, my parents weren't 'lovely-dovey.' Did that give me a pass to make bad choices? Absolutely not. It gave me opportunity to see things from a different perspective and realize that because God is within me, I have everything I need within me. The attention, validation, and reassurance that I sought from others was never going to be enough if I didn't see it in myself for myself.

GOOD VS. EVIL

We all have a choice. This reminds me of a well-known Cherokee legend that highlights the conversation between a grandfather and his grandson. The grandfather explains that he has two wolves inside of him. One wolf is evil filled with greed, envy, hatred, arrogance, and darkness. The other wolf is good filled with generosity, hope, love, humility, and light. The grandfather tells his grandson that these two wolves battle inside everyone. The grandson asks which one wins, and the grandfather replies, "The one you feed."

I believe the same is true for our lives. There's good and bad in every circumstance, but we have power over which one we feed. Whatever we speak to, nourish, give energy to, and focus on is what is going to grow. Are we going to allow the negative circumstances we face lead us to more toxic choices?

Or are we going to allow ourselves the opportunity to learn from those experiences? Reflection and crying have allowed me to acknowledge my thoughts and actions and gave me the courage to endure the process in the middle. At times, I was treated unfairly. At times, I was wrong. I felt broken, tired, lonely, unsure, disappointed, and scared so that's what I dressed in as a result of feeling lonely. I fed those feelings. I had a pattern of having a new experience, facing adversity from it, and then trying to rush to the end of it to feel better or to free myself from the pain it caused. I repeatedly jumped from the beginning to the end of every situation and the same results kept occurring because I wasn't enduring the process in the middle. In addition to that, I was also feeding my fears. I gave life and energy into the negative things I'd experienced which is why the same toxic behaviors and patterns continued to grow in my life.

I eventually stopped rushing through the middle of my story. I slowed down, listened, and learned. I asked God to bathe me. To wash me in His truth because I was tired of dressing in clothes that no longer suited me. I was tired of feeding myself substance that didn't nourish me. It only left me empty and depleted.

I had been wearing hand-me-downs of generational curses and ugly patterns that I'd been too afraid to separate myself from. I'd been hiding in costumes designed to keep me hidden, and the spiritual part of me was tired of the shame, hatred, bitterness, and jealousy I was wearing every day. That part of me decided to stay in the middle so that I could wear something else without forgetting whose I was and where I came from. I was carrying the same bags from story to story and because I always had them at the beginning and never unpacked them in the middle, I had always ended up with the same stuff at the end. I wanted to travel lighter, and prance around in my freedom dress. I wanted to hold my head up and smile, knowing my Father adores me. That's the truth I wanted to feed myself.

In the middle of my loneliness, I opened my hand to accept the fancy, new wardrobe my Father had for me. Now that I wanted to be fully clothed in His armor, I knew I'd look better, feel better, and smell better. I knew I'd dance to a new song with a joyous melody.

Loneliness helped me realize that I needed to change my clothes and what I was feeding myself in the middle of my story. So, ladies, what are you wearing? What are you feeding yourself? We must keep reflecting on these questions. If you don't like what you're wearing, what do you want to wear? If you don't like how you 'smell,' what's going to change your fragrance? What is the new narrative on your playlist?

Loneliness is going to visit you. Are you going to just rush through the visit so that it's over, or are you going to see what you learn in the middle? Are you going to open yourself up to that process?

This revelation for us isn't a one and done. The affliction, temptation, and challenges will get real, so the journey will definitely be a work in progress. We might have moments when we will reach for old stuff. We may think it's clean, but it isn't. Sometimes loneliness may have us dig in the garbage just to see if there's anything we missed. We might think, "Maybe we'll find something that shouldn't have been thrown away." Like maybe it fixed itself with time, so let's just double check since we still have access to it. Like, maybe he's better so let me see what's up. SMH.

Those thoughts we had can resurface and when they do, what are we going to do? For me, I must choose to be grateful. I must go into reflection mode, and this is when I break out one of the millions of journals I have. I take the time to write out what I'm grateful for which causes me to shift my perspective. When I think about what I must appreciate, I start to feel different. Not that the circumstances changed, however, my attitude about it has changed.

When we are intentional about trading negative vibes for positive ones, we will find that appreciation makes the heart feel better. It changes our entire surroundings when we focus on just being thankful. Does it ever make you feel better? How about when you document your revelations? Sit still in the middle of your story and feel every emotion. Write it out. Process it. Cry it out.

For many years, I worked in customer service and people would always be quick to complain, but never to compliment. Even as a consumer, I notice that we usually take the time to grumble. When something isn't right, or when we're not satisfied or happy, that's when we'll send an e-mail to the corporate office. Negative experiences usually spark a fire in us to make the experience known, right? Well, do we give that same energy to provide a compliment? Will we also write a letter or send an e-mail for a positive experience?

Is it the same in our personal lives? I noticed that my journals were filled with bad stuff. I'd write an entry when 'shit hit the fan'. I never took it out when I was blissful, and I had good things to report. If that's you, too, then let's challenge ourselves. Let's not only talk about what's wrong and what we don't have, let's also talk about what we can appreciate. Let's reflect and celebrate what we're grateful for in our lives. Let's just see how shifting that energy impacts how we feel.

Our truth – there are things that we're lonely for or lonely because of in our lives. The void of what's not there will be deafening to our ears because it's so loud. However, our appreciation and revelations about our experiences can speak louder if we just let our voice be heard.

REFLECTION:

In this moment, what can you celebrate in your life even when you feel lonely?

Chapter 8
Intentionality

When I got sick and tired of being sick and tired, I became driven to be intentional about some things. In the spring of 2013, I knew that I couldn't do life alone anymore. I knew that if I kept up with the cycle of work, home, church, and home, I was going to lose my mind. Against everything in my willpower, I decided to join a small life group at my church. To my surprise, I enjoyed the company of others. We talked, shared, ate, laughed, cried, studied the word, and prayed. At the heart of our time together was fellowship, friendship, and food! We were different ages, but through my encounters with them, I learned the power of sisterhood. It was an amazing feeling to have somewhere to go every other week other than home.

My life shifted even more that same year in September when an ex friend invited me to a bible study. Yep, she was an ex friend because she had left our church abruptly and walked out of my life earlier that year. I never thought I'd see her again. I had known her since 2002 and back then, she was my hero. I admired her and she was the role model and mentor I wanted. She was beautiful, talented, and smart, and I felt like she was a celebrity in our church.

While engaging in the deepest level of toxic behavior this time from someone who was COMPLETELY off limits, I had no choice but to accept an invitation to a meeting from this ex friend. I went to the bible study, but I couldn't really talk to her. She had hurt me a few times before, so I was cold to her. My fear was wide awake this time and my guard was up.

I showed up to the bible study out of obligation and obedience, but I was numb. She could tell that I was standoffish and guarded, but she was prompted to invite me to something else. In September of 2013, she birthed REAL Women Rock. It was a sister circle that provided a safe space for women to do real work on themselves. I finally went for the first time in December and at first, I was just there. Every month, I just kept going. Not really believing in it with my whole heart, I kept going to my small group at church and to REAL Women, and guess what? GOD met me there and He changed my life!

Just in taking the small step to say yes and show up, I found something. I found me! I uncovered who Keah was and is, and who she wants to be. I began to heal, grow, and change. That ex friend became my real friend again and I finally let her love me. I finally let myself love her. And from afar, she watched me grow up. She made me a part of her team. I found ways to help her with her women's organization and before I knew it, I was walking in my purpose which was tied to her purpose. She was the one 'pregnant' with a vision and I watched her birth it, and watched it grow up. I ended up being an auntie again, but this time, not to a real baby, but to a movement that would essentially move me. I was filled with things I never expected. Being connected to her in that capacity got me 'pregnant' with a purpose, too. As a result, I went from being a silent participant to a lead facilitator. I began to help empower women to be their best selves as I evolved into a better version of myself.

Sisters, I shared that story to let you know that being intentional changed my life. I couldn't keep living the same way. So, for those of us who are like Samantha, sometimes we're the ones who will have to reach out. Yes, we'd love for our friends to make plans with us and invite us to something, but if that hasn't happened in a while, I encourage you to take the initiative.

For the Victoria's and Mariana's out there, we know it's your heart's desire to be a great mom. You're living your dream and you just want the best for your children. You want to be there for every activity, every event, and every moment. But just know super mom, it's okay to live for you too. Schedule a playdate for your babies, but from time to time, girlfriend, schedule one for you too.

As a mom, you have this divine opportunity to show your children what self-care looks like. Let them see Mommy enjoy some 'me' time so it's not foreign to them as they grow older. Instill this value in them now and consider practicing it as a family. Show your little ones how meaningful and freeing it is to invest in their hobbies and interests. Model making this a priority as you figure out how to balance this with the obligations to your family.

I once heard in a Commitment 101 sister circle that we as women are usually last on our list of commitments. As a mother, you have so much to juggle on your list, and it won't always be easy, but if you don't take care of yourself, you won't be able to take care of everyone else effectively. And learn how to address the guilt that you may feel when you can't show up for every event for your child. This may be a beautiful opportunity to allow aunties, uncles, godparents, and grandparents to be present in the lives of your children. Embrace the village who is there to support you and give them the chance to act in their roles.

Natasha, your husband works so hard because he wants to be an amazing provider for your family. I pray that you will believe that the same husband who provides for you is the same husband who will listen to you. Just because you assume he's busy, overwhelmed, and stressed doesn't mean that your desires and wants have to be suppressed. We are all guilty of faulting others for not giving us what we want, but have we really asked for it? Have we really made it clear what our wants and needs are? Maybe your husband thinks that shopping sprees make you happy. If it's just him you'd rather have, just tell him. Release it and give power to your voice.

Belinda, you thought you were going to live it up once you retired. But now you don't even know what to do. Perhaps you're bored and you're struggling to find your purpose in this stage of your life. What do you want to do? What do you like? What do you need? You now have the time and space to give yourself your full attention. One chapter may have ended in terms of the work world but pick up the pen and write the next chapter. There's a different type of work to be done now.

LaShay, let your hair down, girl. Those degrees on the wall and performance awards don't keep you company, do they? You want to have fun, aren't you talented enough to create it? You deserve it. Like one of my best home girls says, you can be this AND that. That serious career-oriented go getter can be the life of the party too. The joy is discovering what that is for you. What do you want it to be?

Anastasiya, you've moved to a new location. You miss your old friends, but guess what? You deserve some new friends too. You miss the Chat and Chews? Well, create a new one. The women around you may be waiting for you. Better yet, you know who's waiting for you? YOU!!!!

Tracey, your marriage ended, not your life. Get up and live. It's okay to keep living. It's okay to love again too. In this season, start with loving you. You get to decide what that looks like. You get to figure yourself out and give yourself the desires of your heart.

Jessica, you aren't Jesus. You don't have to be the rock for everyone. You're so busy being there for everyone else, that there's a girl inside of you that is screaming for you to pay attention to her. Answer her. Listen to what she needs from you. Be there for you, and when you need others, ask for what you need.

WHAT DO YOU WANT?

Pride will keep us in bondage, y'all. Sometimes I get so tired of depriving myself. I get so angry at the world for not calling me and asking me if I want to go out, but then I think about it from a different perspective, I ask myself: Who have I called? What event have I planned? When was the last time I texted someone and invited them over or out somewhere?

Remember when I previously mentioned that some of the ladies on my women's kickball team didn't pick me to be on their co-ed kickball team? I told you how hurt I was about that. I cried real tears over it and girl, I felt so bad. It really made me feel like I wasn't good enough.

Okay Keah, so, what's the move? Are you going to just quit? Stop playing kickball altogether because obviously, you're not good enough? I had to make a decision. One that wasn't based off my emotions, insecurities, and assumptions. It would have been easy for me to walk around in my feelings of bitterness about this thing. But I couldn't let this situation lead me back down a path of isolation because who does that hurt? ME! I had to pick myself up and move forward.

There will be many occasions on our voyage when we simply feel overlooked. It's inevitable. However, we can be intentional about making the choice NOT to stay there. Feel it, acknowledge it, and move FORWARD. Keep doing what makes you happy and puts a smile on your face. And make the choice to have a positive attitude. Remember, whatever you give life and energy to is what's going to grow in your life. The weight of hate is so heavy. Wouldn't it be awesome to travel light on our voyage? Wouldn't we feel so much better if we chose to be kind and loving? Doesn't it cost us too much to pout and be nasty? Would we really enjoy our voyage and get the most out or our experiences if we choose to focus on offenses?

If a child at recess came to you and said no one picked them to be on their team, would you tell them to sit on the wall, pout, and be angry for the rest of recess? Nope! You'd tell them to go find someone else to play with and enjoy their recess!

So, on purpose, I didn't carry around hate or anger towards the girls that didn't pick me for the co-ed kickball team. I smiled and continued playing kickball. I continued playing with them in the women's league, and I joined a different co-ed team. There's no bitterness or eye rolling. I let it go and I continued to play. I want to encourage you…keep playing.

GOOD VIBES ONLY

For us to experience good vibes in our lives about whatever we're facing, we must be intentional. Recently, I struggled to get out of bed every morning. I couldn't sleep at night and my body just didn't feel right. I made a doctor's appointment because the pain in my stomach was a bit alarming. My doctor listened to my symptoms and recommended I take medication for anxiety. I said, "No ma'am."

No judgment at all for anyone that must take medication for whatever reason. I take medication for several things myself, but I didn't want to take anything for anxiety. That was my own personal choice. I suspected that I was feeling anxious and overwhelmed, but I also admit that I hadn't been doing anything about it.

The joy of learning about yourself is that you find out what works for you. But there's something else…you must be intentional about actually doing those things. For me, I absolutely love walking. It's relaxing, therapeutic, and, along with the right food choices, it can help keep my weight and my sugar down. But there was a problem, I hadn't walked my butt anywhere in months!

I'd spent the cold winter months laying in my recliner watching Hallmark movies and eating Reese's, chips, and French onion dip. Kickball wasn't in season either. I'd been paying a gym membership that I hadn't used in so long. But to avoid taking medication for anxiety, guess who started walking her butt around the school for 15-20 minutes each morning? With laced up tennis shoes and Chuck Brown pumping in my ear, I started getting it in!

I said earlier that God has a way of getting our attention. This situation got mine. I want to reiterate that I'm not against taking medication, I just knew that I needed to try other alternatives first. I was praying and reading my devotions, but only half-heartedly. I wasn't focused at all. I was checking things off my to-do list.

I became intentional about tapping into what helps me relieve stress. For me it's prayer, counseling, devotions, attending a grief group, walking, journaling, watching the Golden Girls, playing word games on my phone, and scrolling through Pinterest. What is it for you? Whatever it is, be intentional about saying yes to you!

Although they can be painful, annoying, and inconvenient, I am sure that we can all agree that our hiccups as a result of loneliness can move us in the right direction. The potential for us to turn things around and to experience joy as a result of feeling lonely is usually available to us. Something typically happens to spark our attention to it. For me, the very thing that hurts me becomes what drives me.

I'm so excited for us to discover what our intentions are and then learn to acknowledge them out loud and embrace them with open arms. Remember those negative records I mentioned before that I listened to repeatedly? You do the same thing sometimes, don't you? Girl, who wants to dance to that broken record? If we wanna get our groove on, we gotta change that song!

As you discover what it is that you want, think about accountability. Have you identified someone to hold you accountable? Have you made a declaration to at least one other trusted person about what your intentions are? Consider doing so because if you don't, your dreams may continue to be deferred. Time isn't standing still, but you are. If you let it out and speak it into existence, your intentions will now have a voice and be more than just a thought. Let them be heard!

REFLECTION:

What are you willing to change in your thinking and behaviors to achieve or obtain the things you want to have or do?

QUIET SPEAKS

I'm tired. Actually, tired isn't the word. I am exhausted. I've been wrestling for a long time, and I'm simply tapped out. I have spent so much time and energy trying to fix everything. When things haven't moved at the rapid pace of my expectations, I worked overtime to rush it along.

When I had ideas and solutions, I ran with them. I convinced myself that I knew what was best, and I could mend anything with just the right words. I spoke softly, and when that didn't work, I got louder. I yelled, demanding to be heard, and still, no one listened. I even sprinkled some tears in there, and still, I seem ignored.

When words couldn't be audibly heard, I tapped into my creativity and wrote them out. I'd send it in a letter or disguise it in a card. Maybe if it's read, it will be heard that way. But still, nothing has worked. I've tried to get mountains to budge, and they just won't move no matter how hard I push. I thought I was strong enough. After all, the weight of the world has been on my shoulders and my pain has been incredibly heavy, so surely, I can move things.

But, how come it's not working? Why are my efforts in vain? I'm trying and trying and trying, and nothing is happening. Why isn't anything changing? Why isn't anything going according to my plans? I've casted the vision, and now, I'm ready to be the star. I've even taken the initiative to give everyone else their parts. And guess what? I wrote their scripts and picked out their wardrobe. Why aren't they delivering the right lines? That's not what I picked out for them to wear. They don't look the part I want them to play.

Leadership is the director, but no one is following her orders. What else is she supposed to do? She's been yelling at the top of her lungs and she's been pulling and pushing. She is tired of trying and she feels depleted. She's empty. What else can she do? She is losing this battle and her grip has loosened.

Exhaustion sat her down and whispered in her ear...

It's time to let Quiet speak. Listen to her now and just BE QUIET.

Chapter 9
Self-Discovery

To me, loneliness seemed like a battle and I'd often felt like I lost the fight. It had driven me to overeat, overspend, act a fool, wear 'dirty' clothes, and indulge in lies and negativity, but it had also worn me out. It had taken a toll on my mind and my body. It left my spirit restless and my heart with such a void, I sometimes doubted if anything could mend it.

What Loneliness Was for Me

Loneliness had offended me and left me feeling empty. It caused confusion, embarrassment, and it had the audacity to be with me for so very long. The unwanted guest showed up way too often, and she was so disrespectful. If I was receiving karma for something I had done, my hands were up, and I was crying, "Uncle. You win, Loneliness. You got me. You beat me. I give up."

Have you felt this way? Loneliness was a rude oppressor who was abusive and had no regard for our feelings as women who desired companionship. She was a tyrant who bullied her way into our lives and sat right on our chests, pushing us into a discomfort so strong, we felt paralyzed. She had us dressing in the way we felt so we wore garments of shame, oppression, sorrow, disappointment, and bleakness.

For me, Loneliness had caused massive affliction in my life. She ruined my past, still had the potential to destruct my present, and had the nerve to threaten my future. She was crippling, demanding, and dangerous. I HATED her! I was terrified of her!

She threatened my life and had the power to take me out! I had never known something so mean and vicious. She had made me a repeated victim and she had left tremendous marks on me. I couldn't hide the bruises, cuts, scars, and wounds she'd inflicted upon me. They were a part of me, and everyone could see them. It was even detected in the sound of my voice.

When I stopped wrestling with loneliness, she got right in the face that she'd previously punched many times before, and she made me look straight at her. She puzzled me and I could barely see her through my tears, but she commanded my attention. This aggressor straddled me, and I couldn't fight her anymore. She trapped me. She moved to my ear and revealed that she had a secret for me. She expressed that she'd been wanting to introduce me to someone.

Startled and confused, I asked, "Who?"

Slowly, intently, she whispered, "You."

Loneliness put the purpose in my pain. Me, someone who had nothing to say. Someone who insisted that married pastors should stop preaching to singles about enjoying their singleness. Someone who shook her head at mothers who told childless women to be encouraged and just wait. Someone irritated with social butterflies who told introverts to go out and "Do you, Boo." Someone with a little girl still inside of her who begged for love but who didn't know that it existed within her all along.

What Loneliness Is to Me Now

Now, equipped with the capacity to love, honor, and own my truth, I can stand firm, tall, confident, and assured. I have made peace with my reflection and I have forgiven myself and my pain. I have owned my part and understand the root causes of my actions. This awareness enables me to acknowledge, accept, and adjust.

I was the woman who menstruates every month like clockwork but would only feel like a true woman if I birthed my own child. I was a childless mother.

I was a friend who missed friendships. It was me that wished the phone would ring or who wanted my friends to just show up to keep me company.

I was the teacher who didn't like planning alone. I was the teammate who longed for a team. I was the mentee who wanted to be mentored.

I was Keah, the girl who wanted so badly to be pursued that I tried to control what that process looked like, sounded like, and felt like. I wanted it so badly that I tried to direct it, and then I justified my manipulative behavior with not knowing any better because I wasn't accustomed to it. I used loneliness as the excuse for my repeated offenses.

I was the broken, daddy-less daughter who wanted love from her dad. I reached for the attention he was no longer here to give. In his life, he was too broken to provide it. In his death, it was too late.

I was a spoiled brat who required more attention than it was even possible to give. I wanted, I needed, and I took. I rejected and then blamed others for not trying hard enough.

I accept – I saw her. Keah, the one who was broken and lonely, but there was some life in me. I had taken quite a beating from Loneliness, but I was still breathing. I saw someone who had the ability to be more company to myself than I'd tried to be. I saw someone who knew exactly what I wanted, but selfishly blamed others for depriving me of it. I saw someone who blamed fear for everything, while knowing all along, I had the tools to comfort myself.

At times, I felt solace in looking pitiful, because I was familiar with it. But I hated that presentation. I rarely dressed in a smile and settled for a serious armor instead. I learned to live with the conflict, and I switched masks skillfully. I became a master pretender because deep down inside, I knew I had the resources inside of myself to change.

I complained about hardships and growth all because it made me uncomfortable. I whined and put myself in situations where I could continue to be the victim, in fear that victory would make me seem arrogant. So, it was always someone else's fault for not choosing me when my guard wouldn't allow me to be selected anyway. When would I learn to choose myself?

But I'm not mad. I understand me. I have begun to listen to all of me, and I seek to understand rather than to be understood. I sit with myself now and breathe through my anxiety. I'm learning to work with, and not against, me.

I'm adjusting, listening, learning, and growing. I speak words of life and affirmation because I understand that my energy has the power to produce growth. I have stopped dashing to the end to feel 'un-lonely' rather, I ride the waves of the process in the middle. Uncertain of what it may consist of during this process, I understand the significance of waiting and trusting.

Along this journey, the revelations and self-discovery I've experienced came as a result of God's intentionality in my life. Through the lonely seasons I faced, God gifted me with His company. His words to me. His hand on me. Him opening my eyes to the toxic behavior I no longer wanted to engage in. The lies and negative self-talk He wanted to tear down and rebuild in truth and love. The isolation He wanted me to invite Him into. He captured me and showed me who I am and reminded me who I belong to.

Loneliness often made me feel that I lacked so much in life. I felt void of everything I thought I was supposed to have, and I felt barren. But when I chose to shift my perspective, I felt awakened by unconditional love and fullness. Even in the physical loss of my parents and grandmothers as they now all reside in Heaven, I feel inspired. The hardships I've faced implanted lessons in my heart, shifted my mind set, and because of this I carry them in my spirit. Through reflections from a positive lens, I'm walking in trust and truth. I feel guided and empowered by the legacy within me passed down from those who raised me. I feel nothing short of abundance and I'm walking in it even when I feel lonely at times.

In life, we all face good and bad situations. Everything that happens to us is stored in our memory files, on the hard drives of our hearts and minds. We naturally keep records of every event and encounter we have. Some experiences in our files seem absolutely heartbreaking and traumatizing. Although those are never the ones we'd choose to rewind and play back, we can't erase them. They are a part of our internal system. But sisters, rest assured, we have other memories stored in our files too. Memories of love, hope, protection, peace, promise, and light. Although the 'bad' ones surface now and then, we can walk in confidence knowing that we have protection from those memories. We survived them. They taught us lessons and prompted hearts and attitudes of gratefulness and wisdom. We can spend our energy and effort dwelling on all that was negative and painful. We can keep records of wrongs and play narratives of everything that was bad. We can keep those playlists on repeat if we want to. I've done that and it led me right to a bunch of harmful choices.

At some point, I decided that I wanted to dance to a more upbeat song. Once I realized I had the power to change the record that I continued to play. I reached into my memory files for the good stuff. I shifted my energy to all that was positive. Since our words have power and connect to what we believe, we can be intentional about what we declare.

Ladies, we can stop fighting with loneliness and playing repeats of the sad narratives its impressed on our hearts. We understand that we're going to meet her in many stages and seasons in our lives, and when we do, we don't have to wear ourselves out trying to battle with her. Instead, we have the power to embrace loneliness and allow it to achieve its purpose. It's never to harm, but always to teach.

Loneliness can be the guide to help us discover so much about ourselves. The good, the bad, and the ugly. When we stop seeing her as an abuser, we can finally learn from her. We can acknowledge, accept, and adjust our behaviors and responses in order to make the necessary changes according to her lessons.

Just as there isn't one single cause for feeling lonely, there isn't one solution on how to cope with it either. I understand that your loneliness may stem from reasons other than mine, and I want you to know that I see you. I am thinking of you. However you have responded to loneliness in the past, and how you respond to it moving forward, my prayer is for all of us to experience growth and healing that will propel us into being who we are created to be. I am rooting for us to walk in wholeness and truth with our masks taken all the way off. There will be no shackles on our feet or around our wrists, as the chains of shame, guilt, resentment, and darkness will be broken. We'll hold our heads up high, proclaiming that we are light and are walking in life even in the middle or our journeys.

Maybe we felt lonely yesterday, we might feel lonely today, and we may again tomorrow. But how we greet our loneliness is what matters. When she visits, we can allow her to dress us in bitterness, sadness, disgrace, lies, negative self-talk, isolation, and toxic behavior. Or we can clothe ourselves in God's truth, self-care, self-love, affirmation, joy, freedom, purpose, revelation, intentionality, and self-discovery as we welcome her to teach us whatever her purpose is. How are you going to respond? Just know that you have a choice. When loneliness comes to visit, you can open the door and say, "Be my guest."

REFLECTION:

What have you learned through this journey? What has changed within you? What will still be a continual work in progress?

MEET THE AUTHOR

Keah L. Mason received her bachelor's degree in elementary education from Towson University, and a master's degree in Curriculum and Instruction from McDaniel College. Since 2010, she has worked as a teacher for Charles County Public Schools in Maryland.

As an instructional leader, Keah participated in developing reading curriculum and instructional activities for elementary students. While presenting professional development for teachers in reading, math, and even self-care, she has also served as a trainer and co-chair for the membership committee of the Education Association of Charles County.

Keah is a certified lead facilitator for REAL Women Rock, a non-profit organization that unites women from various backgrounds to connect in a community for the purpose of growth and personal development. Keah writes and edits blog posts, hosts virtual sister circles, and leads a monthly in-person sister circle in Charles County, MD.

Keah is a member of Zion Church where she serves regularly. In 2018, she organized a women's kickball league for Charles County Parks and Recreation.

Keah is one of the contributing authors for the book, *REAL Women on the Journey: A Traveler's Guide for Everyday Life* released in December of 2017.

Made in United States
Orlando, FL
19 March 2023

31185887R00052